REAL SCIENCE RIDDLES

by Rose Wyler · Pictures by Tālivaldis Stubis

HASTINGS HOUSE, PUBLISHERS

New York

What star looks brightest
to an astronaut?

The sun.

The sun is a star. It is the nearest star of all.
That's why it looks so bright and so big.
The stars that shine at night look small because they
are very far away. They are trillions of miles from Earth.

If an astronaut could go that far from the sun,
it would look small and dim.
It would look like any other star.

What weighs many tons
but falls without
making a sound?

Snow.

All the snow that falls in a snow storm weighs many tons.
Millions of snowflakes fall.

The flakes are made of bits of ice with air between the bits.
They are light for their size. They come down slowly
and land without a sound.

What is a caterpillar
after it is
three days old?

Four days old.

It is still a caterpillar.
Some insects never become caterpillars.
Some are caterpillars for a long time.

The woolly bear caterpillar curls up under old leaves
for the winter. In spring it eats new leaves.
It becomes fat and furry. Then it spins a cocoon
around itself. Good-bye, woolly bear.

When the cocoon opens, a pretty moth will come out.

Why doesn't the biggest animal in the world have the biggest feet?

The biggest animal has no feet.

The blue whale — the biggest animal in the world —
may weigh a hundred tons. It is bigger than any dinosaur
of long ago. It is the biggest animal that ever lived.

Look around. It's everywhere.

But you can't see it. It is..........

Air.

You can see smoke in the air and you can see clouds.
Smoke and clouds float in the air, but they are not air.

Air is a mixture of oxygen and other gases.
These gases have no color, so you cannot see the air.

When air moves, there is a wind. Then you see
what air can do.

What can a carrot lift
all by itself?

Water.

A carrot is the root of a plant. This plant needs water to grow. Week after week, the root takes in water from the soil and lifts it up to the stem.

All that water weighs a lot. It weighs more than the carrot.

Strong carrot!

plant

stem

root

20

SILLY SCIENCE TIME

1 **What does a monkey always carry on his shoulders?**

2 **What can a monkey hold in his left hand that he cannot hold in his right hand?**

1 His head.

2 His right elbow.

What has no eye nor ear,
but knows when you are near?

An earthworm.

Night is the time to hunt for worms. See that big one
in the grass. Its front end is stretched out.
Its tail end is in its hole.

Sneak up on the worm.
The worm does not see you. It has no eyes.
The worm does not hear you. It has no ears.

But the worm can feel.
Your footstep shakes the ground a little.
The worm feels this and zips into its hole.

What birds have wings
but never fly?

The ostrich.

The wings of this bird are too small to lift it
into the air. Ostriches grow taller than men.
They are the largest birds in the world.
Ostriches live on the plains of Africa. When in danger,
they run. With their long, strong legs,
they can run faster than lions.

The penguin.

This bird uses its wings as flippers and swims with them. It is a fast swimmer.

Penguins live in Antarctica and other very cold places. They do not fly. When they want to move fast, they fall on their bellies. Then they can slide very swiftly over snow or grass, using their wings and legs to push themselves along.

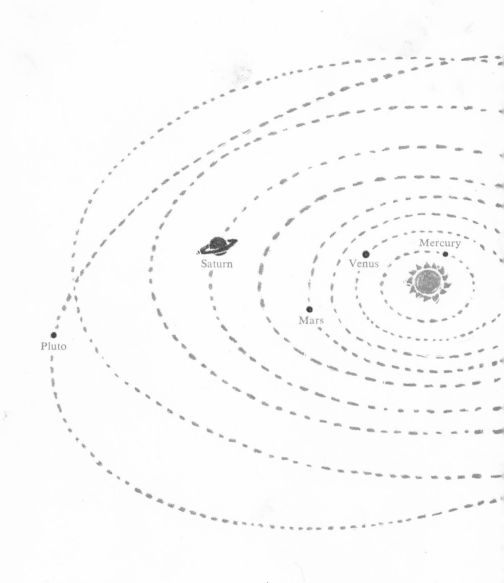

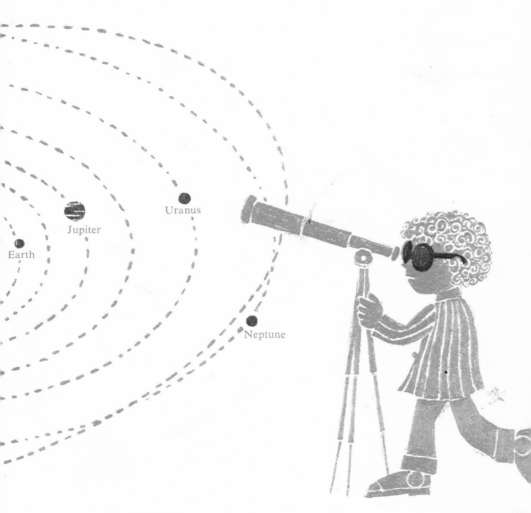

Earth

Jupiter

Uranus

Neptune

What planet do we see more often than any other?

The Earth.

All the other planets are seen only when the sky is dark.
A telescope is needed to find Uranus, Neptune, and Pluto.
But you don't need a telescope to see
Mercury, Venus, Mars, Jupiter, and Saturn.
They look like very bright stars.

You rarely see all five at once.
As a rule you can see just one or two of the planets.

Each planet moves around the sun in a path of its own.
On part of the trip it shines in the sky night after night.
Then the planet goes out of sight for a while.

What has no hands nor feet
but can climb up a fence?

A vine.

Plant a vine and watch it climb.

Take 4 morning-glory seeds.
Scratch a hole in the coat of each seed.
Then soak the seeds for a few hours.
Plant them in a flower pot
and water them every two days.

In a week or so a little plant comes up.
Give it a string to climb on.
At first the plant grows straight.
Then it starts to turn.
It turns around the string,
climbing up and up.

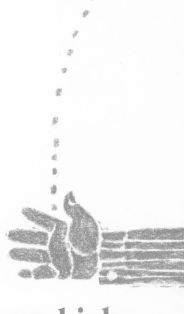

Throw it up high
and it falls to the ground.

Throw it on the ground
and it goes up high.
What is it?

A rubber ball.

When you throw a ball up,
gravity pulls it down.

Wham! the ball hits the ground.
Now it is pushing against the ground.
But that's as far as it can go.
The ground pushes against the ball
and sends it up into the air.

SILLY
SCIENCE
TIME

1 What kind of stones are found in the Mississippi?

2 What can fly under water?

3 What followed the dinosaurs?

1 Wet stones.

2 A fly in a submarine.

3 Their tails.

36

When is an apple like an onion?

Answer on page 40

When is a little girl like an elephant?

Answer on page 41

When you are blindfolded and hold your nose, an apple and an onion taste alike.

Try this test. You will need a tiny piece of peeled apple, a tiny piece of onion, and a friend.

Cover your eyes and hold your nose.
Your friend puts one of the pieces on the tip of your tongue and you taste it. Can you tell them apart?

Now try the test without holding your nose.
What a taste the onion has!
Its smell helps you tell it from the apple.

When she drinks water through a straw.

She sucks up the air inside the straw.
At the same time the air above the glass presses down
on the water and pushes it up into the straw.

An elephant sucks the air out of his trunk,
then water goes up in it. His trunk is his straw.

41

In blackest night

in a dark, dark house,